10

LITTLE RULES
for
FINDING
YOUR TRUTH

by Micki Beach

ISBN-13: 978-0-9974799-5-9

For more information visit www.10littlerules.com

dedication

To Steven, who nurtures my inner squirrel,

to my peapod, who is full of awesome every single day,

and to every living soul who strives to find their truth
regardless of circumstance or their past.

acknowledgements

I humbly bow to all my yoga teachers
who have inspired my journey ...
to Dr. Ray Long for his profound anatomical insights
I so reverently teach ...
to Shiva Rea for uncovering my inner goddess ...
to Kathryn Budwig for teaching me that
"my voice" was perfect exactly the way it was ...
to Seane Corn for guiding my inner rainbow to
become a brilliant light ...
and to all my present and past students who trust
me to lead them in this journey of
self-discovery and self love ...
and my tribe who loves all my sparkles!

table of contents

foreword

I met Micki on the floor of her beautiful, soulful yoga studio about four years ago. I was brand new to yoga, brand new to North Carolina, recovering from major surgery, and unsure ...of everything.

None of that mattered in "The Treehouse," as we all called that space. Micki welcomed me and all my uncertainty with wide arms and a warm smile and I began to heal, both physically and emotionally.

A few months later I gave her a copy of my book "10 Little Rules for a Blissy Life," thinking it might help in some way as she made some major life transitions. We both moved on with our lives.

Life rolled on, she moved away, and I continued to build my 10 Little Rules brand. We reconnected when I moved to Oak Island where Micki had opened her new studio, The Tree of Life. We became fast friends, she welcomed me into her tribe, and she continues to inspire everyone around her, both on and off the mat.

It became obvious that Micki had an important story to tell, and I am humbled and honored that she agreed to tell it through 10 Little Rules. This book you are holding was created with so much love, humility and respect for the awesome power of yoga to both heal the body and deeply touch the heart. May you treasure it as her tribe treasures her.

Carol Pearson
Founder, 10 Little Rules

Micki Beach

the conditioning

I was spiraling….always swirling in a chaotic storm, disillusioned that I had it all under control.

The second child in a big family with an alcoholic, bi-polar mother (cue label "peacemaker"); the emotional sparring partner to not one but two narcissistic husbands (no, apparently I didn't learn my lesson the first time; cue label "door mat"); the elementary teacher turned home school mother and homemaker (cue label "the people pleaser").

I lived my life as if I had to always be everything to everyone. I molded myself into whoever was needed to solve whatever problem arose … to assist, solve, take over, carry the burdens and absorb the pain or discomfort anyone else was having.

I could always "make it better" and ease others' suffering, even as a child. I was everything to everyone … except myself. I often found myself in a puddle of exhaustion due to self-neglect, in both physical and emotional pain. But I never spoke or even thought the words "what about me?" I was never resentful or angry. On the contrary; if people "needed" me, then I held value. I was worthy and smart and useful. So I boldly took on each task laid, or even thrown, at my feet as another feather to add to my plumage.

"Oh, they must think I am great at _____ because they want me to do x, y, z." (Feel free to insert your own bullshit here).

We are taught these are our roles or duties, to be the perfect daughter, wife, mother, friend, employee, boss, neighbor, co-worker … I could go on for days with all the roles we play, all the capes we don. We are taught to be selfless, not selfish. We are taught to be a light for others, not cover them with our shadows. We are taught to smile through the pain, walk it off.

Yet eventually my back grew so heavy with all these capes. I knew somewhere deep down inside me I had a very special gift, a light that flickered at the oddest moments. But I was too busy stirring too many pots and spinning a multitude of plates to listen to those faint whispers. This, that or the other thing was always more important in that moment. Mind you, none of these things had anything to do with my own needs.

Then there is that whisper again … softly, faintly. I'd answer back "Would you just shut up? I don't have time for you right now." "Now" always needed me. It always seemed to require all my attention.

And so we fold in under the weight, we grow bitter (silently of course), we chastise and deprecate and hate ourselves for feeling anything other than fulfilled in our roles. It starts on the inside. It isn't until our body starts to speak to us, insistently, that we even begin to heed the warning signs. The back pain, insomnia, weight gain, migraines … (insert your own symptoms here).

"Everything is fine," I'd lie to myself. "I just need to rest, or maybe walk it off."

My ex-husband told me, after I shared my weariness and pleaded for his help to shoulder some of these burdens, "Someone has to be a grown-up, Micki. Someone has to work and make money and be responsible. Someone has to be the adult."

In other words, this is exactly what my life was supposed to look like. This WAS my life. I chose this. How can I complain? This became my mantra, repeated so often it became an endless tape in my head.

So I curled up my mermaid tail and packed it away in an old dusty trunk and went back to cutting the fat out of my budget, cooking healthy dinners, and sending my RSVP to that purse party.

I went on with my chosen life.

Micki Beach

the catalyst

Eventually, my body began to scream at me. My back hurt so badly I couldn't sleep, which made me mean and angry and easily frustrated. My feet hurt all the time from my time spent teaching on public school concrete floors. I was losing my spark. My sparkles. They were literally seeping from every pore. I found it hard to even muster up a smile most days.

I began to wonder, with a cold shock of fear, "What if I'm not what everyone needs me to be?"

I had based my value on how full of awesome I was to each and every person who needed something from me, I couldn't see my worth outside of their needs.

On the unsolicited advice of too many people, I eventually found a Pilates class. "You need to strengthen your core then your back won't hurt," I heard from friends. I guess they got tired of me complaining and tried to help.

They had no idea how very powerful that one statement would become to me. That revelation — I need to strengthen MY CORE — and the insight to follow would have a profound effect on my life.

So here I go into my local Pilates class (the most ungraceful person you will ever meet. I can fall three times walking UP the stairs). I rationalized it wasn't dance class or a demonstration of my graceful skills (of which I had none). All I had to do was lie on the floor, do six to eight of one exercise, then move onto the next. Even I could do that, in the back of the room of course.

Several weeks later to my utter surprise, my Pilates (super spy-like now revealed to me as Yoga) teacher unrolled a yoga mat out in front of me.

"What?"

"No really ... what?"

Not able to illicit a response from her, I wanted to smack her, which slowly evolved into the sensation of wanting to kick her in the spleen. She half smiled. She knew ....

I actually laughed out loud at her; as she proudly displayed this "thing" as a gift to me, her eyebrow raised in response. Shit....she KNEW!!! My capes began to come loose from their sacred knots around my neck. One. By. One.

She wants ME to bend and twist and show her all my physical and metaphorical PARTS, let alone the ungraceful disturbance I would cause to the class?

My weaknesses, my vulnerabilities, my pain, my history — MY TRUTH. I had heard the stories of yoga, what it was all about, what it expected of me.

She half smiled again and pushed the mat a little closer to me ...

I resisted the urge to rip that raised eyebrow off her face. Then my Type A, control freak self slammed on the panic button. The laundry list of excuses spewed forth.

When the rational mind finally re-emerged, the excuses mentally depleted, I thought, "Well, it is just exercise, I can stay in the back and go unnoticed. They keep the lights down low right? I WILL get stronger (have you seen those women on the magazine covers? I'll take those killer legs and ass, why not?) I will sleep better, no more insisting on foot rubs from an exhausted husband, no more complaints of back pain...

"OK, I can do this." I professed it proudly. Besides, I had tons of capes right? I could just gather back the one I would need; I'm sure I had it in this pile somewhere. I'd take what I needed, and just leave all that other spiritual "stuff" they offer to those patchouli wearing, non-shaving, tree hugging hippies.

So I stepped on the mat ...
and I cracked wide open!
I found ME ...
my heart's speakings.

Once the storms were stilled ... I heard my truth, my purpose ... and those killer legs and ass I had envisioned?

Well ... that no longer mattered.

Micki Beach

RULE #1
Be Still

How often are we really still? The breath, the mind, the body, all still at the same time? We wear multitasking like a badge of honor, yet how often are we ever truly present to any one thing?

I can wash dishes, consult on homework, plan a dinner party and its corresponding grocery trip while I am paying bills … all at the same time. This is no great feat for the modern day woman. More so, it is expected. How did we move from a generation of women where nothing too significant was ever expected of us because we were thought to be incapable, to the expectation that we had superpowers? (That little voice whispers "you asked for this.") We all know those moments when our family looks to us to conjure up a lost shoe and magically prepare dinner in 17 seconds while we wave our wands and put everyone's clean laundry in its respectful places. Right?

The only nudges we typically get to bring us back to the present moment are usually discomforts, aches, pains even, in our bodies. (Mine wasn't so much a nudge as a slap upside the head before I recognized my own needs.) They were those slow rubs on my lower back as I transitioned from one task to another, or the wrenching of the neck to feel just how tight it really was. These are the voices of our self-neglect, our lack of mindfulness, our outward push instead of

RULE #1
Be Still

our inward pull. They were finally speaking up... and loudly!

Slowly, our vitality fades, our spark, enthusiasm, our life force ... and with it, our safety, our grounding, our security. Somehow this physical nudge plants emotional seeds of self-doubt and fears of inadequacy.

"I should be able to/used to be able to do all this," we say to ourselves, wondering what's happened. While we are trying to be everything to everyone, we lose our tether that safely binds us to our uniqueness and true value. The physical pain and discomfort are the first signs our bodies give us that something is wrong.

What I first learned on the mat is that most of us have little to no concept that we are more than the labels we assign ourselves or accept from others. We are more than mothers, sisters, employees, or someone's wife.

If all those things ceased to exist at this very moment, YOU would still exist.

Stop for a few moments and think about that.

Now that you've found a pace other than warp speed, take a moment to stand. (Or, maybe you're already standing because you're doing 14 things while you are reading this.) Take off your shoes and put your feet to the earth. Spread your toes, then rock a bit back and forth. Come back to center and distribute all your weight equally in the balls and heels of your feet. Be still ...

Resist the urge to name what you feel; just allow it to exist.

Lift your toes and firm your legs. Once you feel your strength, release your toes back to the earth and keep that strength in the lower

RULE #1
Be Still

body. Do you feel the warmth growing?

It's like plugging ourselves back in.

This gives us a moment to step back inside ourselves. Now press your feet outward (without letting them actually move) and feel the stability your outer thighs provide. Let your tailbone drift down.

Be still...

This area around the sacrum is where we store our emotional pain, our hurt, all the insecurities, our sadness and anger. This primordial root is the energy center, where we first evolved at conception. Our energy began dividing from here, forming into cells that nurtured our spinal column all the way up to the head, long before our vital organs began to develop. This is the genesis of our existence as a human being.

Exhale deeply and feel your tailbone drift down. Draw that strength and warmth from the legs up into the belly by imagining there is a string attached to your navel and it is being gently pulled towards the spine. Imagine that string now lifting up into your spine. Grow taller. This sensation may be overwhelming the first time we find it, empowering, maybe even selfish as we take this opportunity to feel and acknowledge our own strength.

Level your chin with the earth and own this strength. It is yours. It has been with you all along.

Be still...

POSE #1: Mountain Pose

Breathe … Inhale … Exhale slowly…

1. Come to standing
2. Align your heels under your hip points
3. Begin to supinate (roll outwards) & pronate (roll inward) the feet
4. Lift the toes off the floor to activate the thighs
5. Lower the toes but keep the thighs engaged
6. Press down into your feet and outwards, without allowing them to move
7. Allow the tailbone to float down
8. Pull the navel towards the spine, then draw it upwards
9. Roll the shoulders up, then back, then down
10. Reach thru the top of the head and with the chin level with the floor, drift it back slightly

Now in your mind repeat …

"I am enough."

Imagine your feet growing roots into the earth, your source of this strength and renewal. Draw your hands and this energy up into your heart and hold that space for as long as you need to.

Feel you.

Be still.

Now listen.

your turn ...

Be Still

Take a moment and meditate/ruminate/reflect or pray on these questions:

1. What are the labels you've assigned yourself or others have given you? Write them in the pages that follow. (You probably need the rest of the book pages to write that list, right?)

2. Next, take a typical day and list all the tasks you might perform at the same time or one right after the other without pause.

3. Plan today to take 10 seconds to yourself to "Be Still" as you transition between every task. Commit to this stillness for one week, then come back to your journal pages and reflect on what you have "heard."

date _____

Be Still

date _____

Mountain Pose ~ Tadasana

date _____

Be Still

date _____

Mountain Pose ~ Tadasana

Micki Beach

RULE #2
Expand

Being still can sometimes inflict an absolute sense of oppression. It's like everything hits you all at once, and it's overwhelming. We busy ourselves with all the external pulls so often that when our bodies are finally still enough to speak to us, our brains start telling us everything that is wrong with taking this time to be still. The logical mind starts to reel at this new quiet of the body, and rebels.

My mind refutes a bit like this:

"Obligations are being left unattended."

"Tasks a, b and c are waiting (see their feet tapping?)"

"Everyone else's needs only grow when I turn my attention inward."

"I am selfish, self-centered, and have no right taking time for myself."

That old mantra creeps back in: "This is what I signed up for; I chose this life; I allowed all these labels of mother, wife, friend who will help with anything."

More often than not, the logical mind wins and guilt pervades, so I grab my list of sticky notes and get back to work. We dare not dig in our heels and focus on what we need, because we are marathon runners built to last, worthy of that gold medal. Standing still is not in our play book.

Yet this conflict of re-tethering our roots and finding our strength,

RULE #2
Expand

claiming our power, throws us off balance. And it's not just us who gets thrown; if our child or mate or boss walked in at that very moment, they would call for the straight jacket because we aren't moving at our typical warp speed.

"What's the matter with you?" they ask, not because they are concerned about us, but because we are throwing a wrench in the works. Worse yet, they see us still and assume we have nothing to do, so they ask us for even more help, adding to our non-stop pile of sticky notes.

Our conditioning has taught us to "tread lightly," "don't rock the boat," "please others," "don't make them uncomfortable," "smile and be happy." And like magic, that logical mind allows the "center" we've just found within our place of stillness to dissipate like it had no meaning. Yet it created a ghost image on our body and mind; our heart recognizes its meaning, pausing just long enough to plant a seed of self-love and nourishment. Once it's been planted, our heart will long for even just a tiny moment of that stillness again, that calm space in the storm, that warmth and power in our bodies. But where do we go from there?

We must expand.

Our tendency in those quiet stolen moments is to reflect. It's not the heart-mind that speaks first but the one that sits above those heavy, burdened shoulders that has the loudest, most demanding tone. We begin to chastise ourselves, we berate our outward image (how could I have let myself go like this?), we recount our failures and the people we've let down, those tasks that went uncompleted.

In order to avoid that guilt from our "failings" we look to our outer shell and start making more mental lists ... usually more "to dos" like purchase gym membership, get hair appointment, stop eating x, y, and z. WE become our own next project list but only to the point that

RULE #2
Expand

it doesn't interfere with anyone else's needs or plans. Most often it is only because we need to be more attractive to our mate, less embarrassing to our children, more professional for our jobs, more of whatever the role calls for.

It will take you many tries and much more effort that you can image just to master Rule 1. Yet it is from there, my friend, that everything blooms.

So let's try it again.

Re-root yourself. Be still ... really still. Turn off the logical mind for a moment and every thought that comes into your head, and tell yourself instead ... Inhale ... Exhale ...

Now reach your hands to the sky. Spread your fingers and let your tailbone drift towards the earth. Press your feet outward again slightly and soften your shoulders. Lift your chin a bit and look up. Remove your protective armor and be vulnerable for just a moment. Allow the light from around you to permeate you and fill all those dark places you have kept hidden so long. You are safe. You are rooted.

Now expand ...

POSE #2: Extended Mountain Pose

Breathe … Inhale … Exhale slowly…

1. From your rooted Mountain (Pose #1), with your feet pressed into the earth and your hands at your heart, draw your energy up your legs
2. Take a deep inhale breath
3. Release your hands from your heart and let them drift down to your sides
4. Press your palms into your outer thighs and then backwards, without allowing your hands to move
5. Feel the stability this creates in the upper body
6. As you exhale let your tailbone float down a little more
7. Breathe in again, and turn the palms up
8. Sweep your arms to the sides and up to the sky
9. Keep the shoulders relaxed
10. Allow the palms to face one another, spread your fingers and reach through your hands

Now in your mind repeat …

"I find focus and purpose in expansion."

Look up. Allow your throat and heart to open.
Sometimes expansion starts simply with taking a full breath and releasing the physical heart space.

Feel you.

Expand.

Now listen.

Take a moment and meditate/ruminate/reflect or pray on these questions:

1. What "speaking" do you hear from your "logical mind" as you open up your body?

2. What self-chastisements rise to the surface?

3. Are you fearful to expand in your own direction, away from your current "role"?

date _____

2

Expand

date _____

Extended Mountain ~ Urdhva Hastasana

date _____

②

Expand

date _____

Extended Mountain ~ Urdhva Hastasana

Micki Beach

RULE #3
Reflect

Expansion is intimidating. Maybe you felt that in the last chapter. Did you find yourself peering over your shoulder to see if anyone was watching?

We are used to folding in, protecting, shielding and ignoring our heart's desires, its quiet whispers. Yet true expansive release cracks open that tiny seed our stillness planted. That seed has always been with you, lying deep in the dark earth waiting to emerge. Maybe your seed is a bit like mine was; it loves the security of the darkness.

Does the comfort of a big, nice house or fancy car appeal to you ... protect that seed? Mine was safe, held in a sacred space far away from my duties and roles and labels. Even my emotional scars from childhood trauma padded and shielded that seed. It's as if they were saying "nope, no one is even getting close to this."

Initially what we hear is from the mind instead of the heart. We can change this dynamic through the common yoga position of a forward fold. By folding inward we place the head below the heart, effectively putting the heart in charge of the inner dialogue.

It is amazing to me that this one simple folding posture can alter so much within us. Our negative self-talk is no longer the main focus ... the heart is now in a protected space and becomes dominant. In the vulnerability of this inward turning, we can begin to truly reflect.

Think back to those labels you noted earlier. Are they self-

RULE #3
Reflect

-imposed? Are you overextending yourself to fill a need, or to fill a void? For years, my relationship with my ex-husband most days resembled two roommates doing everything they could not to irritate the other. We "conferenced" on what bills should be paid. We discussed our daughter's calendar and who was responsible for what. Household and food duties fell to me because I didn't have "a job," even though I home-schooled our child.

I felt the expectations of me even if they weren't stated or demanded, yet I see now I placed even more expectations on myself. He often told me, "I don't care if you cook. I could eat a turkey sandwich every day." I mistook this statement for compassion, a sign that he understood my overwhelming load of tasks, roles and capes. So I tested it. And yes, he absolutely did eat a turkey sandwich for more than three weeks … with a smile. He really didn't care!

He didn't care if his underwear was washed, folded and put away they moment it hit the laundry basket. He did not care if dinner was on the (perfectly set) table when he came home from work, or if the floor was swept four times a day to keep the pet hair under control. It was all me!

I have no idea how this June Cleaver imposter took over my body but I was convinced it was for the happiness of a smooth running household. Everything had its place and should be put there promptly.

As my forward folds evolved and I was able to get past the screaming in my hamstrings and actually relax and breathe, my head began to relax below my heart … and this is what I heard …

"You have to be the perfect wife so you are worthy of this great man."

"He 'allows' you to stay home and home school your child, so he deserves to be taken care of."

"You can't do anything else anyway; you only have an elementary teaching degree." (Remember the old saying, "Those who can't …

RULE #3
Reflect

teach.")

Then I took a deep breath in. I exhaled with a deep sigh.

I thought I was content. I thought this was the life I wanted. Little did I know this was the literal mind trying to hijack the heart again.

All that blood drawing up from my strong legs coursed through my heart and down my spine and back into my brain. And this is what I realized in those moments of protected reflection:

I've always needed to control everything. My home was utter chaos growing up. It was a daily task to dig through the laundry basket to find something for my brothers and sister to wear that didn't smell of mildew. Being "needed" was a way I could control the situations cycloning around me.

I do have a job! One so important and least recognized yet invaluable to the future of our nation. I was raising a child to be an intelligent, independent, resourceful, compassionate and creative human. This was no 9-5 job I could come home from and kick my feet up with a beer and watch TV until dinner was ready. It was a full time, non-stop job. Every waking moment was (or so I thought) about helping this child develop into the best version of herself. But I was letting all my capes smother the most important one, the one closest to my heart.

My talents are beyond measure. My ability to inspire and teach and nurture are true gifts. This realization made me breathe a little deeper and sigh just a bit louder … and the rest started rushing in.

I realized I was capable of amazing things. I realized I was worthy of good things. At the same time I realized any pleasure I sought for myself was blocked by the shame of my childhood. I realized I took

RULE #3
Reflect

the blame for any and every little thing that went wrong, and carried that burden like a torch to light my way. (Just throw one more cape on my back. I can bear it.)

The realizations came quickly once I let my heart lead the conversation ... and what it told me changed everything.

POSE #3: Forward Fold

Breathe … Inhale … Exhale slowly…

1. From Extended Mountain (Pose #2), hinge at your hips and fold to the floor

2. Your hands may not reach the floor and that's fine. Simply place your hands on your thighs or shins, wherever allows you to breathe comfortably

3. Press your feet down and outwards and feel the hips ignite

4. Gently draw your navel to your spine to protect your back

5. Wherever your hands are resting, press them down

6. Gently begin pressing the hands outwards as well

7. If you can, add one final adjustment of pulling the hands towards your belly (remember, don't let them actually move, just press in that direction until you can feel the muscles engage)

8. Allow your neck to lengthen by slowly reaching the crown of the head towards the floor

9. Keep a slight bend in the knees to allow the back to decompress a bit more without straining the hamstrings

10. Hold this pose, breathe in and out, with a few deep sighs on the exhale

Now in your mind repeat …

"I am worthy and capable."

Rooted into the earth, take a moment and feel the energy circulating from the earth thru your feet and up your legs. Allow that energy to move down your spine. Let it release your shoulders as you sigh deeply. Let it course through your arms then into your hands as you offer it back to the earth.

Feel you.
Now listen ...
and reflect on what you hear.

Micki Beach

your turn ...

Reflect

Take a moment and meditate/ruminate/reflect or pray on these questions:

1. Who did you have in your life that you emulated growing up? A parent, teacher, church leader? Why did you look to them as role models?

2. What "beliefs" do you hold about your roles, your tasks and duties?

3. What realizations did you have about your roles when you reflected inward?

date _____

3

Reflect

48

date _____

Forward Fold ~ Uttanasana

date _____

3

Reflect

date _____

Forward Fold ~ Uttanasana

Micki Beach

RULE #4
Accept

This rush of true realization quickly becomes a purge, and this purging of the soul can be exhausting. The emotional release of all the burdens and pain we have carried for so long can be overwhelming. Sometimes we even lack the willpower to move even a step forward.

Yet we somehow find the way to keep moving.

I never felt the true weight of those capes I wore until I realized it was in my power to release them. And in that release, the emotion can be immense. You may have experienced those moments ... maybe you've had a gut-wrenching cry with your best friend. Sometimes the purging appears as an impromptu sing along to the car radio so loud someone can hear you three cars over. Or maybe it is an off the cuff rant over a parking space or a slow driver. Releasing our emotions leaves a hollowness in our chest, an unfamiliar space in our belly. We are so used to the "fullness" of energy in our bodies in constant propulsion that when we find some "out-of-character" way to release it, it leaves a void ... a raw, empty void where that anger, sadness, guilt or longing once resided.

Maybe if we think of this space not as a void but a place of stillness, a quietness where we can listen to our heart as it speaks our truth, our "purges" may begin to happen with less drama, less guilt and shame, and more acceptance of the beautiful change we are

RULE #4
Accept

witnessing in ourselves.

Acceptance of what we uncover when that tiny seed bursts open puts us on the path to healing. But we must find our inner power to navigate that path. We can only find the path to our truth by walking through all of our pain.

My labels as wife and mother were so honorable to me. I had vowed to become the exact opposite of what my mother was. But at what price? The pressures I placed on myself and my family were keeping us all on edge, as I used my quest to be the perfect wife and mother as my way to "undo" my childhood pain.

I started to really hear how I sounded when I ranted about some unimportant thing.

"You did not just walk in the house with your nasty shoes on? Now I have to sweep AGAIN. Seriously!"

My pain turned into agony when I realized my behavior was silently teaching my child what kind of mother and wife to be for her family ... a critical, controlling, unhappy perfectionist.

I had to accept that the expectations I held myself to, that I allowed others to hold me to, were absolutely exhausting me. I had to accept that I was not perfect (my mind's voice already knew this, and was relentless telling me so, but I couldn't let anyone else see it). I realized that the energy and perceptions I was sending out into the world were just getting boomeranged right back to me ... usually smack dab in the forehead!

Amazingly, as the fire grew in my belly, all those scars I held on to, sheltering that seed, started to burn away. It forgot about my fear of feeling out of control. The fire grew and burned away the shame attached to my imperfections. Fueled by this power, my true self found its voice ... without the labels and sticky notes and capes and exhaustion. Those whispers were no longer quiet ... hearing them felt like an old friend coming home. She wrapped her arms around me and

RULE #4

Accept

held my tender heart while it cracked wide open. I had to accept that every stone I had laid in building my future was mined from the quarry of "the daughter of a crazy mother."

I had spent the better part of my life striving to be better than my mother ... even better than the few "gifts" she allowed us to see when she was relatively well and would spend the day baking or painting or planting in her garden. Yet those gifts turned into challenges; I was always chastising myself for not being a better gardener or baker or painter than she was. Now, instead of being critical of myself, I worked at being a better friend, who always loved and listened like she'd never been capable of doing. I held my child longer and met to her needs more attentively, so she would realize how important she is to me. I began to believe there was a different way, that life is about nurture over nature.

Because we are so used to side stepping conflict, glossing over and smoothing contradictions, we rarely "own" what we find. We simply shove it a little deeper when it rears its "ugly" head. Our self speak tells us "no one will understand. It's just me. This is my problem and I have no right to complain."

Our truth knows better.

POSE #4: Plank Pose

Breathe … Inhale … Exhale slowly…

1. From your Forward Fold (Pose #3), step your feet back to the rear of your yoga mat
2. Make sure your hands are under your shoulders
3. Spread your fingers as wide as you can and press into the first finger knuckle
4. Draw your navel to your spine as if a string is attached to it and someone is lifting it to the ceiling
5. Press the floor away with your hands to create a slight arch to the upper back
6. Keep the elbows facing toward the back of your mat
7. Slowly start to sink thru your heels but keep your hands engaged
8. Press down into your hands and try to slip them forward without allowing them to move
9. Drift the tailbone down towards your heels as you lengthen through your neck
10. Feel free to place the knees on the floor if needed, but keep your belly engaged

Now in your mind repeat …

"I accept and embrace my imperfections."

Draw your power from the earth up through your hands. Keep your fingers spread and palms flat as you slightly round your upper back drawing your overextended heart back inward. Firm your legs, and gaze down between your hands.

Feel you.

Now listen …

and accept what you hear.

your turn ...

Accept

Take a moment and meditate/ruminate/reflect or pray on these questions:

1. What form does your purging take? Are you usually alone or is there someone you feel safe to release with?

2. Take a moment and imagine that all those "heartstrings" you constantly extend outward are being drawn back in to fill all those cracks around your own heart. Which cracks around your heart need tending to first?

3. Are you comfortable enough in your own power to accept the healing that will come forth? What resources do you have to support you along the way?

date _____

4

Accept

date _____

Plank Pose ~ Phalakasana

date _____

4

Accept

date _____

Plank Pose ~ Phalakasana

Micki Beach

RULE #5
Release

With a fresh understanding of our heart speak, we take a moment to humble ourselves. Look inward. What are you feeding your soul? Do you feed it a diet of old habits … quick fixes … a frantic pace? Do you wrap yourself up in to-do lists … self-loathing … anger … resentment?

When we soften our belly to the earth after Plank Pose (Rule #4), we can feel the sensitivity that resides there. Does your belly feel soft yet stable? Sometimes it's hard to release the belly, having been trained to protect that space for fear of metaphorical sucker punches. Are you constantly on your guard? Are you waiting for the next shoe to drop?

I lived my whole life in fear. Fear of the future … the next five minutes and next week and next year. This fear turned me into a perpetual planner. I had to know every detail, every second's movement and all scenarios that could possibly go wrong. My ex-husband was passive aggressive so my sucker punches came in the form of cynicism, sarcasm and a never-ending depletion of the last square of toilet paper every time I went to the bathroom.

Something was always missing, misplaced or just "wrong" and needed to be fixed. Little did I know that it was usually by his making. I had so many expectations of who I should be that I actually assumed he took on the male variation of the same role.

RULE #5
Release

I assumed everyone took life as "seriously" as I did. That everything I thought was important was equally as important to them.

The realization that absolutely no one cared about x, y, or z saddened me. I didn't want praise ... ever ... I just wanted someone to care as much as I did. When they didn't it was like a punch to the gut.

Then I thought ... if they cared as much as I did then they wouldn't have outsourced the task to me, right? (Add one more cape ... she has a strong back).

Releasing my expectations of others was extraordinarily hard, nearly insurmountable, yet not nearly as hard as releasing the expectations I held for myself. The roles I had "chosen" ... did I really have the right to pass the torch, or simply not take it up? Would anyone care about this project or that role as much as I did and really do it justice?

I slowly realized that I couldn't be everything to everyone, everywhere, all the time. I had to just let some of it go.
But my release did not come all at once. It started with baby steps, in my obligations to friends.

Lord knows, we southern women love our home parties ... purses and makeup and kitchen gadgets and candles. I was invited to a different home party at least once a week. I graciously went and browsed and handled and looked interested and asked all the pertinent questions. I even took out my checkbook and bought something. Never the cheapest item either; I had to show I cared about the hostess' success (I had to, right?), even though my budget could in no way afford it. I carefully made a mental note of what would be sacrificed later. (I would use a green sticky note for that one!)

Then ... oh my gosh ... then, one of my massage therapist/yoga friends approached me. She knew I could never say no (cue "doormat" label). She gushed about how my home was the perfect place to host a Botox party.

RULE #5
Release

Are you freaking kidding me? I looked at her dumbfounded as she continued her coercion by explaining how my yoga friends would love it and she could get us all a discounted rate and, and, and ...

I felt like someone donkey kicked me in the chest, and I could feel the heartstring I had extended out toward this friend reel itself back in. Did this woman, a close friend of mine I thought, not know what my evolving yoga practice meant to me? I was learning self-love, self-appreciation, self-acceptance ... and Botox? I thought surely she must be joking. Clearly she either had no respect for, or no understanding of, the path I was on, or anyone else on that journey with me for that matter.

It was something I rarely said, but now the word NO hissed from my lips. I believe at that moment the angels did their dance rendition of "Can't Stop the Feeling," hip thrusts and all. And suddenly I felt power surge up from my belly and become this warm fuzzy around my heart. And to my surprise she simply said ... ok.

From that point on, I did not attend another party to buy something I didn't need ... ever!

That was the first step to releasing the standards I held myself too as "friend." Sometimes it's a biggie. Sometimes it's small steps, taken one after the other.

If we keep our hearts open for the opportunities to let go of what does not fill our cup, to release what does not serve, we begin to honor ourselves and let go of the burdens we carry, without explanation and without apology. (And I had no doubt that Botox would not serve any part of this body or budget!)

POSE #5: 8 Points Pose

Breathe … Inhale … Exhale slowly…

1. From your Plank Pose (Pose #4), drop your knees to the floor keeping your toes turned under
2. Keep the elbows drawn in towards the ribs as you slowly lower your chest to the floor
3. Look forward and place your chin on the floor, or your forehead if there is too much compression in your neck
4. Press the tailbone skyward
5. Allow the space between the shoulder blades to soften
6. Let your heart sink towards the earth
7. Keeping the palms grounded and fingers spread, attempt to spiral the hands towards the outer edges of your mat
8. Allow your throat to soften
9. As you inhale, pause just for a moment at the top of that inhale and feel the chest expand
10. Give your tush a left and right wiggle to release hip tension

Now in your mind repeat …

"I release my past so I can embrace my present."

We must humbly release any anger or pain we hold in our heart space in order to find healing. Feel the power in your hands, the deep arch of your back. Feel the freedom on the pelvis and the strength in the shoulders. Allow all that you have been carrying slide off your shoulders and down your back. Then wiggle your tush to shake it all off. Have fun with this pose. Then come to a place of stillness.

Feel you.

Now listen …

and release what doesn't serve you.

your turn ...

Release

Take a moment and meditate/ruminate/reflect or pray on these questions:

1. What "scars" from your past affect your decision making in your day-to-day life?

2. Why do you hold on to this pain? Do you feel it is your burden to bear? Why?

3. If you let go of this pain, would it create room for something else that may need to grow?

5

Release

date _____

8 Points Pose — Ashtangasana

Release

date _____

date _____

8 Points Pose – Ashtangasana

Micki Beach

RULE #6
Replenish

When we start releasing things from our life, we sometimes feel a void or empty space where it used to reside. As tempting as it may be, we must not allow ourselves to curl up in this space and long for what was there to return.

As a very smart friend of mine wrote, "Forward motion is all that is required." (from 10 Little Rules for a Blissy Life)

Who knew? We feel like we are always moving but how often do we check in to make sure that movement is in a direction that nurtures our soul? Now that you have found time to slow down and consider, reflect on and accept your heart's speakings, what will fill your spirit? What will fill those "voids" you have created by releasing what did not serve you?

Have you even considered what nourishment YOU might need? Maybe, like me, you don't feel like you deserve this nourishment and nurturing for your own soul. We are so used to making sure everyone else's cup is brimming over that we can't even find our own cup anymore.

Many people have rituals that help replenish them … that morning cup of coffee or a long run after work. Take a moment today to notice how others fill their cup. Really pay attention to people as they take time for themselves. I bet the majority of them are on their phones or writing notes, making their next "to do list," juggling that smoothie on

RULE #6
Replenish

the non-stop stream of errands. Even when we are doing something "for ourselves," we are taken over by multitasking.

Now think about the things that truly fill you up … think about what you were doing during a time when you felt nurtured, safe, loved and relaxed. These feeling may have been triggered by subtle actions, so take cues from those around you.

Someone once noticed how I was always rocking and mentioned this to me. That was my cue. I went out and bought the coziest rocker I could find and put it on my back porch, where my dog liked to lay in the sun and I could pet him with my feet. I put a small table beside me to hold my big glass of chocolate milk (another favorite from childhood) and a favorite book, overlooking my garden filled with beautiful flowers and a pond where our "adopted" pet duck liked to swim.

I had ignored all these nourishing things for so long … I had even avoided sitting on the back porch due to the uncomfortable, conservative straight back chairs our family had picked out. I was missing out on all this nourishment because of a chair. We don't need extravagance; our nourishment can come from the simplest things … things that draw you out of your logical, multitasking mind back into the present moment where the deep breaths emerge.

As I became more aware, simple things filled me back up, which led me to noticing how safe "being calm" felt. I started taking long, hot salt baths so my sleep became less restless. I perused consignment stores and waited for some form of beauty to inspire me. I bought the few craft supplies I had longed for and started "creating" handmade journals from recycled books because I loved to write in them.

Then came those "speaking truth" moments again. I had told myself I wasn't creative or artistic like my mother was on her "good" days, yet here were these beautiful handmade journals I had created when my heart was finally able to be still; journals that my friends asked to

RULE #6
Replenish

purchase from me. This allowed me to confidently trust in my natural abilities. It validated my crafting skills and told me my creativity was more than a flight of fancy or some over-the-rainbow, longed for wish. We must be willing to reflect and accept what our hearts long for … without guilt and in confidence that the "lies" we've been telling ourselves are just a form of self-torturing conditioning. Our true nature always emerges once we start replenishing our spirit, and then the next stone on our path somehow magically appears.

POSE #6: Cobra Pose

Breathe … Inhale … Exhale slowly…

1. From 8 Points Pose (#5), slide the legs back so they straighten
2. Turn and press the tops of the feet to the mat; firm your backside
3. With hands under shoulders, keep your elbows close to your sides
4. Allow the forehead to release to the floor for a moment and pause
5. As you inhale, roll the shoulders towards your ears, then squeeze them together and pretend you are sliding them into your back pockets
6. Press into your hands and begin to straighten the arms a bit
7. As you lift the head, do it so slowly that you feel when the tension creeps in the neck, then ease the chin down just a millimeter or so to release that tension
8. Draw your navel into the spine and drift the tailbone downward
9. Press your pubic bone into the earth and soften your gaze forward
10. Pressing firmly into the hands, attempt to spiral them out again and allow the chest to open

Now in your mind repeat …

"I honor, respect and embrace my authentic self."

Draw the energy up from the earth into your hands and arms. Allow your heart to rise, understanding this physical and emotional vulnerability is an attitude we can cultivate. Feel the power as it surges through you and allow your heart to feel deeply. This place of vulnerability is where we connect and replenish with others.

Feel you.
Now listen.
Replenish your heart, mind and spirit.

your turn ...

Replenish

Take a moment and meditate/ruminate/reflect or pray on these questions:

1. Feel the softness in your belly. What "sensitivity" resides there that is holding you back?

2. What activities or hobbies fill your cup and replenish you?

3. Can you share your talents with others with confidence?

date _____

Replenish

date _____

Cobra Pose ~ Bhujangasana

Replenish

date _____

date _____

6

Cobra Pose ~ Bhujangasana

Micki Beach

RULE #7
Breathe

Observations, reflections, new thoughts and feelings sometimes send us into a tailspin. We may feel skeptical of what we feel. "This can't be right," we may think, because it does not match the conditioning we are so used to referring to as a blueprint to our day-to-day lives.

Or, we react like we just hit the lottery and spin off in a multitude of directions. Sometimes we feel the need to "fix" our lives all at once, or even outright revolt away from all our duties and tasks. We stand adamantly upon our soapbox and profess all our "findings" and expect everyone to care about them as much as we do.

In reality, all they see is a chaotic spiraling that resembles a cyclone.

As you begin to replenish, notice what feelings come to the surface. Do you feel so bombarded by emotions that you have no idea how to put a governor on that gas pedal? As I grew into my true self and out of all my old conditioned roles, I felt like I no longer fit in my old skin, much like a jacket bought too many seasons ago.

I was a homeschooling mother, a wife, a friend available for anything, anytime. Only in my stillness was I finally able to understand that I needed to be touched and held and cared for. This was something my ex-husband was incapable of giving. I began to loathe my matrimonial relationship, despise this life I chose. I wanted

RULE #7
Breathe

to shove it down the garbage disposal with all the other crap I was fed my whole life.

Yet the radiant light that shone so brightly from my child always guided me home like a beacon. She needed me. I knew I wasn't who I used to be, but she still needed her mom. How do I make all this fit as I stretch my wings and change?

As my truth began to emerge, my growth wasn't pretty; it was more like a tailspin. There were craft supplies all over my house, there were so many projects going on at once I had no idea in which direction I was going. I started to reel over marketing strategies (which I had absolutely no experience with at all), how was I going to sell my work and create more, where would I put them and advertise and offer them up to others? (Yep ... I was creating more sticky notes!) All I had done was add to my ever-growing list of tasks to be completed. My cyclone just landed me right back where it had lifted me off the ground.

This was about the time I finally felt comfortable enough in my basic yoga practice to attend a workshop held in Chapel Hill with an orthopedic surgeon named Dr. Ray Long. After cramming into a tiny room with 70 other people, our mats edge to edge, he began to ask us about our yoga practice. I sat very quietly, yet near the front due to my hearing impairment, hoping to go unnoticed. Others immediately chimed out the oft-recited spiritual speakings of the "best way" to move within a yoga practice. He noted their answers, but his gaze kept drifting to me.

He knew.

His knowledge was deeper than the shallow, rote verbiage being given back to him. Because it was so predictable, these ready answers, he knew they were not coming from someone's truth, only words and cues and meanings others had memorized to feel knowledgeable, accomplished, like they were doing yoga "right."

RULE #7
Breathe

He asked us to assume a posture that resembled an upside down V. I did as I was told and waited patiently. He held us in this posture for more than seven minutes. During that time, he began to draw our focus to our mats and our bodies ... first our fingertips, then wrists, arms and shoulders. He drew our minds to our hands, our spines, our belly buttons and then on to our thighs, knees, and feet ... ending with the tips of our toes. In all that time my body was finally able to feel what the posture needed to express in MY body. Not what some teacher told me I should feel. He then explained that in one minute I could take 10 full breaths. And in the seven minutes that we held the posture, we could take 70 breaths, each one deeper than the last. (I couldn't tell you the last time I had even taken five full breaths).

The tailspin slowed, the sticky notes began to fall away onto the mat around me. Having my head below my heart for that long gave me time to be still once again, to reground and release all the pain, anger and resentment I had held onto for so long in my hips.

Sometimes in all this discovery and healing we need to just be still again and breathe. Did your replenishment nurture that seed or create more chaos? Does your seed reach for light, water, nutrients or is it tangled up with all the other roots below the dark, rich earth?

Focus on your heart as you take this posture. What does it tell you? Inhale and exhale slowly. Just stay here and breathe ...

The path will slowly emerge, the distractions will fall away to reveal your truth.

POSE #7: Downward Facing Dog

Breathe … Inhale … Exhale slowly…

1. From Cobra (Pose #6), deeply bend the elbows and lower the chest to the floor
2. Turn the toes under and lift the knees off the floor to firm the thighs
3. Drop the knees back to the floor and drift the tailbone down
4. Press into your hands while bending your knees and sit back towards your heels
5. Lengthen out the arms and reengage the hands
6. Inhale deeply and lift the knees off the floor, keeping the arms straight
7. Balance the weight equally between the feet and hands
8. Keep the navel drawn towards the spine and allow the heels to sink a bit (Keep your knees bent if the backs of your legs are tight)
9 . Allow the ears to rest between the arms as you gaze mid-mat
10. Try lifting your toes to engage your thighs

Now in your mind repeat …

"The breath of life nourishes me."

Begin to pedal the heels in a slow "walking" motion, as long as the breath comes easy. This pose can be overwhelming for some. Feel free to drop your knees to the floor whenever you need a break. Taking the time to get the head below the heart allows the logical mind to take a short vacation and the heart-mind to sing to us. Stay here and just focus on your breath. Allow each inhale and exhale to lengthen a bit. Sigh as you exhale and let the pose speak to you.

Feel you.
Breathe.
Now listen.

your turn ...

Breathe

Take a moment and meditate/ruminate/reflect or pray on these questions:

1. What directions have you been spiraling in since you have started taking time to replenish yourself?

2. Do you feel busier than ever now … with more tasks to be completed? Has your growth become a to-do list?

3. Which parts/duties/tasks in your life make you resentful? Make a list. (You will look back on this with utter astonishment as your yoga practice develops.)

date _____

Breathe

date _____

Downward Facing Dog ~ Adho Mukha Svanasana

date _____

7

Breathe

⑦

Downward Facing Dog ~ Adho Mukha Svanasana

Micki Beach

RULE #8
Refocus

It may be time to repot that seed, my friend. You have nourished its growth, fed, protected and cared for it. Now it needs more room. The leaves and new branches of this tenderling will emerge. We must provide room for growth. In yoga, we call this seed our dharma, our innate gift.

My practice, my re-found stillness in that workshop, made everything so clear. I was doing what I was supposed to be doing. I was still an attentive mother and doting wife, an inspired crafter … but I was also taking time to find those stolen moments to reground and center and still my heart. Yet during that workshop, even with my head below heart, my mind was carefully arranging the columns of to-do lists. I stole these moments to "plan" what I needed as well.

My mind couldn't begin to fathom how to make my journals into to anything worthy of a business.

"What should I do? What will I have to sacrifice and endure to make this happen?"

I thought I knew what I wanted, and now my type A control freak re-emerged to figure out how to get it done. After that momentous upside down posture, Dr. Long asked us to step our feet up to our hands. And we stayed there … again … for what seemed like an eternity.

So I listened.

RULE #8
Refocus

I thought of the times when I outwardly expressed my passions and revealed a "better way" to enjoy life, and not everyone was receptive. I couldn't conceive that my crafting business, my life raft on this new journey, wasn't enough to sustain a living. I didn't understand that every single person out there floating adrift had their own history, their own conditioning, their own stories to tell, their own heartaches and pains. I never realized that all these other women around me were wearing just as many capes as I was and their truth could not be grown by my truth. Maybe my journal business wasn't as sustainable as I thought.

So I kept listening.

I realized the times in my journal making that I was most fulfilled (here comes the heart-mind ... finally) was when I was answering questions about my art. I enjoyed being able to draw the interest of others with something unique. My heart jumped when they said they had a beautiful book that was meaningful to them and how they would love to do x, y, or z with it. I reflected on the smiles and their own eureka moments ... the creativity that my gift had inspired in others. They didn't need my journals ... they needed to be inspired.

I began to feel a warm sensation around my heart. It grew....

I found myself wanting to make time to teach others how to nurture their artistic inspirations. It filled me up to encourage them to choose their favorite old books, the texture of paper that soothed them and conspire with them about what they could create. I longed to show them how they could find a sense of calm when they nurtured their own seed and how it would fill their cup.

My branches began to grow, my seed no longer a tender shoot that needed protecting.

So I listened more carefully.

Then I heard my heart speak loud and clear. I was put on this earth to teach, but I now knew that meant something more than excavating

RULE #8

Refocus

dinosaurs in the sandbox with paintbrushes and little people. I had no idea how to shift my gaze from that, into following that light radiating from my heart in a far off direction.

How do I take my innate gift, this wife and mother, this ungraceful person in the back of the room, and use it to lead and guide growth for others? I thought my "job" would always be teaching children once I was no longer home-schooling my daughter, and maybe making some extra money on a hobby, but as I folded again and re-focused on just me, my gift, my dharma, I realized the journals were just stones on my path ... and the answers began to emerge.

POSE #8: Forward Fold

Breathe ... Inhale ... Exhale slowly...

1. From Downward Facing Dog (Pose #7), take a full inhale breath
2. Exhale fully, bend your knees and look at the top of your mat
3. Without breathing in, take several small steps to the top of the mat
4. As your feet get closer to your hands, it's okay to bend your knees
5. Plug back into your feet, aligning them directly under your hips
6. Allow the hands to rest on the floor, your shins or your thighs
7. Release the head ... even shake it a bit and let the shoulders soften
8. Try bending the knees deeply and let the belly rest on the thighs
9. Straighten the legs and tuck the chin towards the chest
10. Now take your focus inward

Now in your mind repeat ...

"I am peaceful, whole and balanced."

As you step your feet up toward your hands, you connect once again to the energy from the earth. Cycle the energy up from your feet and legs and through your body, back into your arms, hands and earth again. Draw that seed, that core belief, deep into your belly now where your power resides. When we bend into our Forward Fold we are provided the opportunity to look inward at our heart's speakings again. Our nervous system is soothed, so introspection may come a bit easier. Every nerve firing that comes from the brain travels through the spine to every single organ and part of our body. By creating space between each vertebra in a forward fold, we allow a deeper communication within the body.

Feel you.

Now listen.

Refocus on your gift.

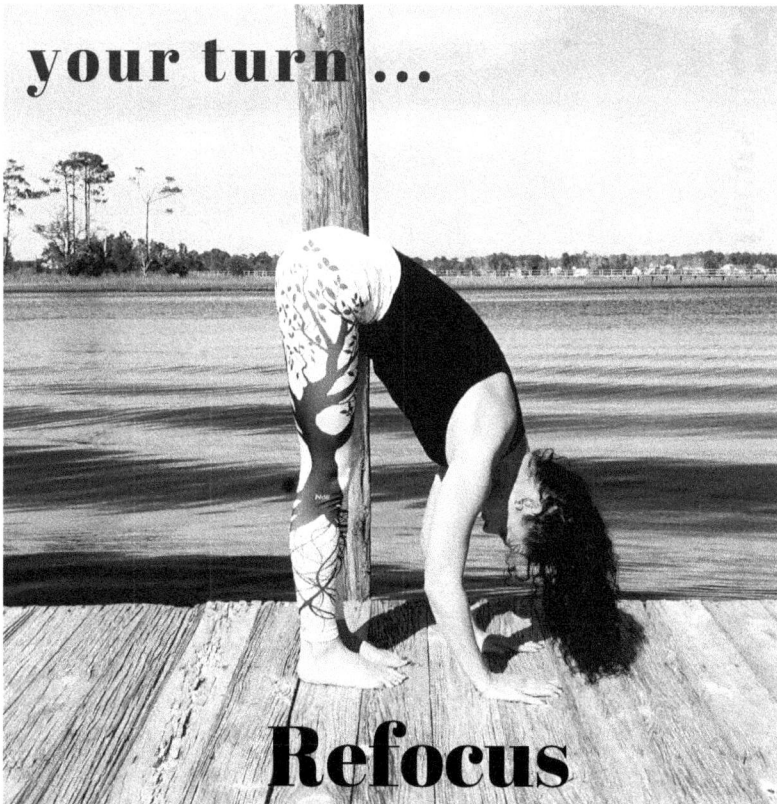

your turn...

Refocus

Take a moment and meditate/ruminate/reflect or pray on these
questions:

1. Can you distinguish your inspirations and talents from your
natural gift?

2. Have you "forced" an inspiration into a "producible" mold in
order to fulfill a conditioned role?

3. Do you feel the need to organize, plan, or structure your gift
to fit the needs or labels of others or to fulfill others'
expectations?

date _____

Refocus

date _____

8

Forward Fold ~ Uttanasana

8

Refocus

date _____

date _____

Forward Fold ~ Uttanasana

Micki Beach

RULE #9
Believe

I often think back to the discovery and emergence of my "seed." What truly transformed my thought patterns, my habits and my roles? When did I start to "feel" again ... what I needed, what nourished me? When did it all shift?

And then I felt it. I KNEW! I straightened my back. I slid my hands up my legs, and reached my heart forward. I metaphorically professed the knowing of my belief, of my truth through the movements of my body. So many times I had heartlessly moved through the yoga poses in what began as a mild form of torture and only progressed to a remedy for physical pain, never realizing that the poses had been speaking through me ... and too me. I just had to turn down all the other noise.

They reminded me each time I moved into them, that I was finally whole ... and even more importantly, I always had been. My thoughts, my beliefs, indeed my very being, were no longer blocked by the attachments to my pain, anger or duty.

I believed in my ability to nurture broken souls like mine, those lost, diverged or misdirected multitasking, plate spinning note-takers. My gift, my dharma, my absolute truth in life and my true duty was to share, to guide others through healing ... in body, mind, and then the spirit. These movements cracked me wide open as first my body, then my mind, began to focus. They forced me to be still enough to

RULE #9
Believe

locate that tiny seed in my spirit and showed me the strength and courage I needed to allow its growth.

I now knew and believed I had the gift to guide others along this same path, stone by stone. I believed I could teach yoga, and help others make profound change in their lives.

I believed. In me. In my truth. In my path.

As I rose to stand (my head above the heart and somewhat empowered again) my logical mind said "you can't do that." My husband agreed, claiming we couldn't "afford" for me to do that. The costs of training, renting a studio, and now the new need of a babysitter, the furnishings and start-up costs … so many logical reasons it wouldn't work.

As he outlined all the reasons it was childish and not respectable, unattainable and illogical (he was reaching for any loose string on my old capes to strangle my emerging new self), my resolve strengthened.

I can and I will. The path will open. The stones will appear.

I knew this! I no longer needed to explain it or make anyone believe it. All that mattered was I believed.

With the mental gymnastics under control, my focus began to narrow. The plan began to emerge. Once I conceived it, it became possible and the Universe started opening all the doors. My multitasking, scattered focus had blinded me from the brilliant light that shone as those doors opened before me in the past … the very same doors I had ignored because I had already one too many things on my to-do list.

Yet there they were, inviting me in still. Seeing them again reassured me I was on the right path this time. I need not force this, or figure out how structure or manage it. I only need the courage to walk towards it … alone if need be, but the only path was forward now.

POSE #9: Half Lift Pose

Breathe ... Inhale ... Exhale slowly ...

1. From Forward Fold (Pose #8), slowly slide the hands up the legs until you can find a flat back

2. Begin to press the feet down and outward again

3. Lift the toes to engage the thighs then spread them as you release them to the earth

4. Remember that string attached to your navel? Again imagine someone is drawing it up to the sky

5. Reach thru the top of your head like a turtle poking its head out of its shell, lengthening the back of the neck

6. Press the palms into the thighs, or down to your shins if you are able to release a bit lower

7. Then begin to press the hands outwards without allowing them to move

8. Feel the power in your back and spine

9. Breathe in deeply

10. To finish your sequence of poses, spread your arms out to the side like an airplane and rise up, reaching towards the sky

Now in your mind repeat ...

"Everything I need is already within me."

Feel you.

Now listen.

Believe.

Micki Beach

your turn ...

Believe

Take a moment and meditate/ruminate/reflect or pray on these questions:

1. What distractions or illusions are pulling you away from your core belief?

2. What self doubt creeps back in? Do others perpetuate this?

3. Are there resources you have yet untapped out of fear?

4. Brainstorm potential opportunities that surround and lie within you. When we put pen to paper it solidifies and validates our purpose.

Believe

date _____

date _____

Half Lift ~ Ardha Uttanasana

Believe

date _____

date _____

9

Half Lift ~ Ardha Uttanasana

Micki Beach

RULE #10
Speak Your Truth

When we become still enough to identify our truth that lies waiting for us in that deep seed, it becomes our core belief. Every step we take should nurture that path of growth. After we formulate and refocus our plan, we must then believe it to be so. We are capable. We are worthy. We are full of awesome!

It is now time to take action. We have cultivated that seed, formulated what we needed to nourish it, refocused and refined and pruned off the sucker branches. Now what?

I finally knew what I wanted and needed, but how do I put that plan into action? Will my support system embrace this me? It takes courage to step into the unknown.

My truth brazenly blurted out when I ran into the fitness director at our local YMCA. I confidently announced that we needed more than two yoga classes a week, taught by an uninspired teacher. I told him I would teach and asked him to find a training class for me … and he did. I became certified and my two yoga classes at the Y became so popular that my students begged for more. The staff told me there was not enough funding for any more weekly classes so my students encouraged me to find another space, any space, just so we could all do yoga together everyday.

Their belief in me, and their gratitude for my gift, gave them glimpses at their own dharma. The next stones emerged and I opened

RULE #10
Speak Your Truth

my own studio doors.

Then more seeds emerged of all shapes and colors and sizes. This "home" I had created ... this safe place for growth and emergence ... nurtured all the seeds until many small seedlings grew. My thriving nourishment grew a tree with many branches and leaves that flowered into such a life-giving energy, our classes filled and more needs surfaced. My studio became nationally credentialed and I was able to teach others how to teach yoga ... and then their branches grew and more seeds emerged again.

This tree that we grew together with heartfelt reverence was called Tree of Life and soon our space was fondly nicknamed The Treehouse. It was and still is a home now of almost nine years, a place of love and self-acceptance and compassion and nurturing. It is my dharma I offer to others, which I had never nurtured or even knew existed until that first yoga mat was rolled out in front of me.

Our conditioning, our roles, our labels do not define us nor reflect our true selves most times. There will always be a formidable force of linebackers (or undiscovered seeds as I prefer to think of them) trying to stiff arm you back into a more appropriate role. These roles are comfortable for them, and it's understandable. Don't forget ... they have been conditioned, and are more likely struggling on some level of their own.

Stay open, keep moving forward on your focused path. Look for those doors cracking open, and they will. Your tribe, the people who truly see your gift, will gather around you and support you, embracing your vision. Those who are blocking your path will eventually get frustrated and step aside, allowing you to move forward if you stay true to your speakings.

Yoga healed me. My body feels better now at the age of 47 than it did when I was 20. It healed my heart, all the pain, longing, resentment, self-loathing and disappointment in myself for settling

RULE #10
Speak Your Truth

for less than I deserved. I love my body and all its imperfections. I believe in me!

I know my strong shoulders can carry much weight. This broad back can carry those in need, and my little Flintstone feet ground me in my stability and strength. All of the "flaws" I once believed kept me from being beautiful, all those cracks in my heart, are just spaces from which my brilliance shines forth.

I believe in me and my abilities, not because someone else makes me feel valuable, but because I know I am valuable. I am a teacher, a healer, a lover and a light. I am an empath and I believe in every part of me and what my body speaks to me. I know my truth. I own my truth. I lead through my truth. Through my truth, I inspire and motivate and encourage others to find their own.

More often than not, our pain and fear of growth comes from not knowing what we will find when we begin the "excavation process," afraid of what the findings will mean, or how it will affect us or others in our lives.

In these 10 rules I simply offer you a set of tools to locate and excavate with. The findings may be ignored or seen as unworthy, wasteful and unimportant; that is up to you. But these tools, like any others, can be used in many ways...

There is a reason you picked up this book, and what you choose to do with these tools is up to you. I simply ask that you honor the practice of yoga by welcoming its speakings and lessons.

How often and with what willingness and motivation you excavate is to be determined by you. The findings, yours alone, to rebury or to take time to clean off and ponder, perhaps even lay reverently aside to continue your search ... they will always be yours. The discovery of your truth lies within this practice.

Be still and know ...

then speak it to the world.

POSE #10: Sun Salutation

Breathe ... Inhale ... Exhale slowly...
Now in your mind repeat ...
"My vision is clear. I express my truth fully."

Feel you! Know YOU!
Inhale and exhale with confidence and courage.
Move through the sequence of these postures you've
learned, allowing the breath to guide each
movement. Anytime your body opens or expands,
breathe in.

When you fold or bend for insight and reflection,
exhale. Be sure to linger at the top of each inhale
and the bottom of each exhale. This is where the
magic happens!

Repeat this sequence of movements again and
again, allowing each consecutive cycle to warm and
encourage you into deeper movements.

The poses will become your path, the stepping
stones to confidently travel on as long as you need
their security.

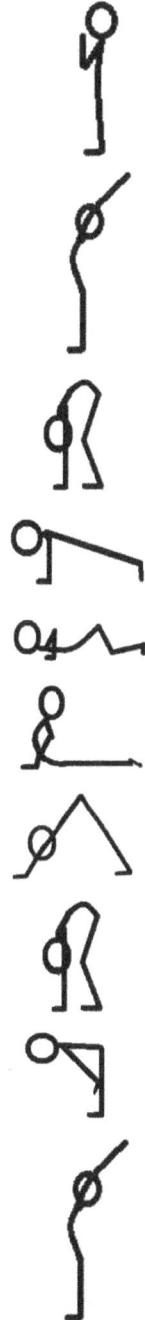

POSE #10: Sun Salutation

When your curiosity and empowerment draws you
forward, move into the next, knowing all the time ...

This is your path.
It is my path.
It is ours.
This is our path to healing and knowing we are all one
... for a better future for ourselves and each other.

May we know our truth
May we speak our truth
And may we always feel it

All the bright sparkly, shiny things in me,
see and honor them in you!

Namaste,

Micki

Micki Beach

Take a moment and meditate/ruminate/reflect or pray on these questions:

1. Every day you practice this sequence it will feel different. What time of day do you find its poses are most beneficial? Why?

2. As we step into our truth, we often feel guilty saying no or speaking up for ourselves. Do you? With whom?

3. Have you been surprised by your heart's speakings? What do you now believe about yourself that you didn't know before?

date _____

10

Speak Your Truth

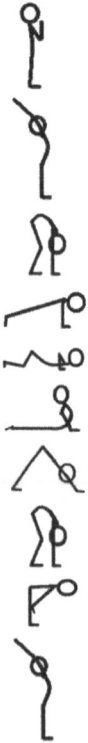

date _____

Sun Salutation ~ Surya Namaskara

10

Speak Your Truth

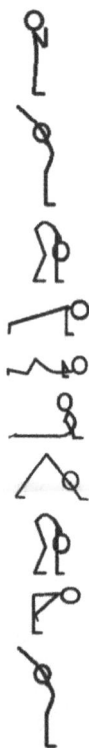

date _____

10

Sun Salutation ~ Surya Namaskara

10 LITTLE RULES
connect with our community

Stay connected to
the 10 Little Rules Community

Like and Follow our Facebook
page at facebook.com/10LittleRules
for ongoing support and discussion on
how to apply these books to living your best life

Visit our website for updates
at www.10littlerules.com

Books in the 10 Little Rules series:
10 Little Rules for a Blissy Life by Carol Pearson
10 Little Rules for Your Creative Soul by Rita Long
10 Little Rules of Hank by Wendy Price
10 Little Rules for Finding Your Truth by Micki Beach

Watch for more 10 Little Rules books launching soon!

www.ingramcontent.com/pod-product-compliance
Lightning Source LLC
Chambersburg PA
CBHW071352090426
42738CB00012B/3090